AF338273

Synchronicity

and

Individuation

Synchronicity
and
Individuation

A Primer of Jung's Analytical Psychology

by

DAVID H. ROSEN

Foreword by Frank N. McMillan III

RESOURCE *Publications* · Eugene, Oregon

To my daughters, Sarah, Laura, and Rachel, and my grandchildren, Aidan, Ben, and Ember.

Also by David Rosen

Henry's Tower (children's book) (Platypus Books, 1984)

Medicine as a Human Experience (With David Reiser) (introduction to clinical issues) (University Park Press, 1984), (Aspen Systems, 1985)

Transforming Depression: Healing the Soul through Creativity (Putnam, 1993) (Penguin Group, 1996) (Nicholas-Hays, 2002)

The Tao of Jung: The Way of Integrity (Penguin, 1996) (Wipf & Stock, 2019)

The Tao of Elvis (Harcourt, 2002) (Rosenberry, 2012) (Wipf and Stock, 2013)

Clouds and More Clouds (collection of haiku) (Lily Pool Press, 2013)

The Healing Spirit of Haiku (With Joel Weishaus) (haiku & dialogue between two old friends) (North Atlantic Books, 2004), (Resource Publications, an Imprint of Wipf and Stock Publishers, 2014)

Lost in the Long White Cloud: Finding My Way Home (1st memoir) (Wipf and Stock, 2014)

Time, Love and Licorice: A Healing Coloring Storybook (Wipf and Stock, 2015)

Darkness Holding Light (collection of poems) (edited by David H. Rosen and Carol Goodman) (Resource Publications, 2016)

Spelunking Through Life (collection of haiku) (Resource Publications, 2016)

Living with Evergreens (collection of haiku) (Resource Publications, 2016)

In Search of the Hidden Pond (collection of haiku) (Resource Publications, 2016)

Less Is More: A Collection of Ten-Minute Plays (edited by David H. Rosen with two of his own plays) (Resource Publications, 2016)

White Rose, Red Rose (With Johnny Baranski) (haiku & dialogue between the authors) (Resource Publications, 2017)

Patient-Centered Medicine: A Human Experience (with Uyen Hoang) (introduction to clinical principles and issues) (Oxford University Press, 2017)

The Alchemy of Cooking: Recipes with a Jungian Twist (cookbook) (Wipf and Stock, 2017)

Samantha the Sleuth & Zack's Hard Lesson (children's book: two short stories) (Resource Publications, 2018)

Opal Whiteley's Beginning and Hoops & Hoopla (historical fiction and personal story)(Resource Publications, 2018)

Torii Haiku: Profane to a Sacred Life (collection of haiku) (Resource Publications, 2018)

Look Closely (collection of haiku) (Resource Publications, 2019)

Warming to Gold (collection of haiku) (Resource Publications, 2019)

Kindergarten Symphony: An ABC Book (children's book) (Resource Publications, 2019)

Lesbianism: A Father-Daughter Conversation (With Rachel Rosen) (treatise on lesbianism) (Resource Publications, 2019)

Every Day is a Good Day (collection of haiku) (Resource Publications, 2020)

Soul Circles: Mandalas and Meaning (With Jeremy Jensen) (clinical treatise with artist analysand) (Resource Publications, 2020)

Torn Asunder: Putting Back the Pieces (2nd memoir) (Resource Publications, 2020)

Soul to Soul: Aphorisms for Life (philosophical work) (Resource Publications, 2021)

Opening Our Hearts (collection of haiku) (Resource Publications, 2022)

Waiting to Cross Over (collection of haiku) (Resource Publications, 2022)

Foreword

His Holiness the Fourteenth Dalai Lama once said "My religion is kindness." Dr. David Rosen's enlightening and inspiring volume, *Synchronicity and Individuation: A Primer of Jung's Analytical Psychology*, is animated by a similar compassionate nature. Indeed, his good cheer is the first thing one notices about him in person. Well, that and his every ready smile, of course, and, above all, his laugh. Hear that and everything is made better. I truly believe that a person never comes away from time spent with David, however brief, without feeling happier, healthier, and more human, not to mention more humane. Truly a healer of minds, souls, and spirits, shining bright as the noonday sun and gentle as a star on a clear winter's night, David radiates an interpersonal light in which I have basked for nearly forty years. You see, David Rosen is my friend, and in every practical way except birth, my brother.

I first met David in 1986 when he came to College Station, Texas to become the inaugural Frank N. McMillan Jr. Professor in Analytical Psychology, a post founded by my late father at Texas A&M University, a sprawling, land grant campus primarily dedicated to engineering, agriculture, and scientific experimentation. An accomplished physician, analyst, author, and artist, David had earlier entered the history of medical research with his coining of the term "egocide" (referencing a revelation that comes to the one percent of individuals who survive suicidal leaps off the Golden Gate Bridge) while he was a resident in psychiatry at the University of California Medical Center in San Francisco (see this volume; he also discusses egocide in his groundbreaking 1993 work, *Transforming Depression: A Jungian Approach Using the Creative Arts*).

Upon assuming the McMillan Professorship, the first full professorship in Jungian psychology in the world, as it happens, David was also appointed Professor of Psychiatry and Behavioral Science and Professor of Humanities in Medicine. What followed thereafter I can only liken to a happy dream; better yet, a happy dream come true. For twenty-five years until his retirement, whereupon he disappeared into the cool, green woods of Oregon like some kind of ancient Daoist sage, there on that campus on the sunbaked Post Oak Savanna, David established an internationally-renowned center for academic research in analytical psychology, a nurturing home for graduate students in Jungian thought who today teach all over the globe, and a hearth for robust creativity in the arts; written, painted, or performed. I can only liken it to a sort of magical, mythical kingdom, as Jackie Kennedy referred to her late husband's administration in her famous December 1963 interview with *Life* magazine, wherein the famous musical's lyrics were quoted, "Don't let it be forgot, that once there was a spot, for one brief shining moment, that was known as Camelot." David's professorship surely seemed so to me, and, in so many ways, it truly was.

Besides an ever-tumbling cascade of peer-reviewed journal articles, books, both popular and academic, and student research that rushed from the scholarly fountain that was David's tenure at Texas A&M, one of the most significant achievements that emerged as a benefit for the worldwide Jungian community was the acclaimed Fay Lecture and Book Series. After conversations with David, the late Houston philanthropist Carolyn Fay endowed a lecture series modeled on Scotland's prestigious Gifford Lectures to complement my father's professorship. Her Fay Lectures, and its attendant book series published by Texas A&M University Press, brought the world's most preeminent analytical psychologists to College Station every April for three-day weekends rich with deep thought, delicious food, good wine, and boon companionship. Camelot, indeed.

And so now, ten years removed from that kingdom on the prairie, the sage lives in his cottage in the glade with his beautiful bride, Lanara, a tender of gardens and champion of nature and all her children. However, one can hardly call David retired. Not really. Actually, he is anything but that. Deep into the night, gazing out onto Lanara's tidy orchard from his study window, he continues to ponder and make his art. This present volume dedicated to explicating two of Jung's most important concepts – synchronicity and individuation – is only the most recent in a stream of prose and poetry that issues forth from those enchanted woods at the foot of the Willamette Valley. And to further mine the Arthurian vein, David there in his woodland refuge, beyond his Buddhist compassion, beyond his quiet, Daoist balance wherein he thinks his "right thoughts that effect change a thousand miles away," reminds me of nothing so much as a modern Merlin, who in an age beset with plague, ignorance, and violence, dreams his gentle dreams, practices his healing arts, and there by the yellow firelight in his alchemical laboratory conjures scientific knowledge that illuminates the path of fellow seekers along the Way. He does this "Work" for all of us. And, best of all, he is my friend.

Frank N. McMillan III
Corpus Christi, Texas

Preface

Thank you to Frank McMillan III for writing the foreword. He has always seemed like a spiritual brother and his family like a second one for me. I was embraced by his parents, Frank and Mabel, who also welcomed me into their home. Later, they welcomed my three daughters as well, for which I will be forever grateful. I recall that Frank III was born in the same city that he now resides in. Oh, Corpus Christi! (which means *the body of Christ)*. And it's not by accident that the McMillan's have similar traits of selflessness and kindness. The joys of family gatherings and trips to the beach are memorable. The McMillan's changed my life when I became the McMillan Professor of Analytical Psychology at Texas A&M University. Little did I know then how significant that endowed professorship would be. However, after twenty-five years of research, teaching, and presenting papers at conferences around the world, I am humbled by their generosity and support.

At my age of approaching 80, I've reflected on critical things we do during life. Play is the first one. As adults, we usually focus on work. However, the essential aspect of growing up is play. For instance, when we go to a new trail in a forest or to a beach with the waves lapping, we do not go into a work mode. We circle back to earlier times when we played. This got me thinking about how both are essential to growing up, and to life itself. It's a balance, which is often forgotten until you go to Las Vegas. But playing slot machines and cards is not the kind of play I'm talking about. Hence, it would be much better in later years to find an unknown path that you could hike on or visit a bay that has not seen a human being in a long time. It would take some work to find these new vistas but it would be rewarding. Why is it important to venture into unknown territories on unused pathways? Because that's how we discover new things and return to our childhood memories and play that we once enjoyed. At some point, we stop observing children's play, which would be extremely instructive for us. Children's rules in their creative games are fair, which is important to remember. Their adventures involve excitement and a mixture of danger and safety. It's really hard for adults to play because there's a notion that we should be grown up. But if you reflect on it, we're actually growing down. It's an unusual concept to think about growing down but it happens to everyone, and it will happen to you as well. Essentially, I'm saying that children have wisdom that we old folks can emulate if we want to. In other words, be open, play, create, go for a walk, paint a painting, and get new ideas. All of these things will promote health and well-being, and of course, a well balanced life.

This work is holistic, or as George Engel called it, biopsychosocial. Each section of this book will be an aspect of psychotherapy or, even going deeper, psychoanalysis. Having worked with Engel in the early 1980's, his views are dear to my heart. My own interest and love of life and biology, which is the study of life, drew me to become a physician, like Jung. As a physician, the physical is always focused on, but what Engel brought to light is that the same must be done for the psychosocial aspects. I once asked him, "What about the soul?" because I had wanted to add the spiritual and soulful aspects as well. He replied, "It's there. It's part of psychology. 'Psyche' means 'soul' in Greek." So, what he was doing, was integrating the soul without specifying it. Engel originally outlined his bio-psychosocial approach in a 1977 article published in *Science*, which really put him on the map. By being with him, as he was a physician, psychiatrist, and psychoanalyst, I got to witness how he integrated all the various aspects of wellness and illness. I identified with him because I, too, am a physician, psychiatrist, and psychoanalyst. We also became friends, so he would invite me to his house where I met his artistic wife, Evelyn, who was a painter. He also introduced me to the roses he grew in his garden. Influenced by him, I also now raise red, white, pink, and yellow roses with my wife, Lanara. What a delight! Engel was a unique individual and meeting and working with him was an acausal connection, which is what synchron-icity means. Another example of synchronicity in my life was meeting Lanara on a bench on the south island of New Zealand, overlooking Governors Bay. After the first walk I took with her, I wrote a small poem:

> What joy
> finding you here:
> small, purple flower

I later gave it to her, which mystified her. However, I felt that she was special and beautiful. She was also delicate and I could tell from her words and her original desire to be a dancer that she was extremely talented and creative.

George Engel and Lanara both manifest the concept of individuation by being their own individuals and fulfilling their personal myths. Another illustration of this was Frank N. McMillan Jr., (who endowed the professorship in Jungian psychology I held at Texas A&M) and his son, Frank N. McMillan III. Frank III, like his father, manifests his personal myth. Once, in a discussion with the older Frank, I implied that he must have been in Jungian analysis. His response was that he had not but that he had read all twenty volumes of Jung's collected works, which surprised and impressed me. He called Jung "the old man", meaning that he felt there was ancient wisdom that came through his work and spoke to him. He then added, "Jung saved my life", and I could relate.

I mentioned the personal myth earlier in order for each of us to focus on why we're here, what we're doing, and the mark we're making in civilization. People don't realize that this is true for everybody; we all have this ability and mission. Often people are afraid to stand out and to make their mark. However, if you contemplate on this, you'll get quickly to the questions: "What is this all about?", "Why are we here?", and "What do we do?". The personal myth brings this home. After each of us is gone, relatives and friends will reflect on what the essence was of our personality and contribution to the whole. A friend might say, "She was committed to fairness and balance." A grandchild might say, "He was curious and fun to be around." And it's even more than okay for the grandchild to win at chess, as mine have, since they are at the beginning and the grandparent is at the end. This reminds us that Plato was right, "The beginning is the most important part of the work." That's why we are drawn to prefaces and forewords. It's sort of like the beginning impression that we make and get when we meet a new person and have a meaningful discussion.

Principle Elements of Jung's Psychology

The Healing Relationship

All healer-patient relationships focus on helping patients resolve problems. My contention in this book is that synchronicity and individuation are at the heart and soul of all transformation! When a patient contacts a healer about a problem or an area of growth or development it ironically relates to the healer. The reason I'm a psychoanalyst is that we are destined to examine our own problems so that they do not interfere with the patient's issues. However, often there's a connection that is unknown at the outset. Harold Searles wrote about how the analyst is also helped when a patient contacts the healer. Henri Nouwen, Carl Jung, Sigmund Freud, Alfred Adler, June Singer, James Hollis, and Linda Leonard all express similar ideas when talking about the wounded healer. The wounded healer archetype is related to myself and anyone who does this work. It is critical to receive the same help you are providing. In other words, the therapist or analyst must deal with his or her own problems, which is the basis of in-depth therapy. I once wrote an article titled "The Inborn Basis for the Healing Doctor-Patient Relationship" which concerns this very issue. The healing relationship is rooted in biology, expanded in psychology, and expressed in a social way. I want to also add the concept of gratitude to this work. How fortunate we are to examine and treat the patients as well as our own lives. As mentioned above, seeing disturbed individuals helps our own troubled souls.

Transference and Countertransference

Transference is exactly as the word implies. It is what the patient transfers onto the therapist, or other individuals, places, or situations. Often it is positive, but it can be negative. For the most part, the patient is unaware of this transference. In fact, the therapy is helping the person be aware of this fact. For instance, when a patient sees me as a super positive influence, that primes my awareness that this is something that is probably not owned by them.

I once saw a poet who had not realized that he actually was one. In asking him to share his poetry, he found it hard to believe that I would be interested. Nevertheless, he brought it into the next meeting and read it. I was struck by the importance of his writing. I even suggested that he could probably get it published in *The New Yorker* or some other magazine. However, at that point in his career, he couldn't believe that. Fortunately, later, he did. At the beginning of therapy, he projected onto me, as his therapist, a goodness that he hadn't yet attributed to himself.

Countertransference refers to the therapist or analyst's transference onto their patient. As with transference, countertransference can be both positive and negative. In the instance described above, it indicates me seeing what my patient was doing as valuable, creative, and worthwhile. However, I have had other experiences which turned sour. For example, many years ago a young woman had an erotic transference toward me and I had the same countertransference toward her. I presented the situation to a supervisor and we both agreed that I should stop seeing her. She felt rejected, but we were able to find her another therapist where these feelings did not occur. It is important for the therapist to embark on a journey of developing insight into their own issues and problems so that they don't interfere with the patients healing, but rather can support the patient's healing, personality, and true self; in other words, the patient's personal myth.

Confession

It takes courage to confess one's problems and issues. However, that's what psychotherapy and psychoanalysis are all about. Confession, as we all know, is religious - meaning that it's bridging a connection to another individual. Psychotherapy and in-depth analysis came from confession and religion, which is not usually acknowledged. However, we all know that we feel better when we confess. And surely, the Catholic church observed and realized that this promoted well-being.

As an example, a middle-aged married woman who was depressed came to see me and she disclosed that she was in a state of despair but didn't know why. At the core, she was dealing with an autocratic father and some family secrets. Ironically, she was an academic, just as I am, which brought home some of my own issues. Often, patients are struggling with human difficulties that the healer is also dealing with. I was struck by her courage in disclosing and facing conflicts that one doesn't usually talk about with others. It helped that we both were academics because I could understand her world and she could understand mine. As part of Jungian therapy and analysis, one shares dreams and active imagination. Active imagination, which will be discussed and illustrated later, is a creative artistic product based on conscious awareness of one's inner conflicts. These activities were new for this individual. However, it was healing, and led to new insights and discoveries. Each time she would come she would bring a piece of art that she had made which we would then discuss, often leading to new memories of old conflicts. This activity is central to overcoming one's depression. Initially, she had told me that she didn't do artwork. However, I reminded her that when we were very young, we all did artwork. She reluctantly agreed, which, as mentioned, became part of the in-depth work.

Equally important to confession is education, which allows one to draw out the essence of oneself through therapy, friendship, memoir, and active imagination among other things. In the case of this woman, through her dreams, our therapy, and her active imagination, she was able to manifest her essence and bring that into her life. Confession and education lead to transformation, which is often a return to and manifestation of one's personal myth.

Conscious and Unconscious

Conscious refers to awareness. It's the way our society tends to operate. We're aware of such things as our relationship and our work. However, we're usually not aware of our unconscious, because we're not-conscious of it. To discover our full reality, we must delve deeper into the unconscious. Common ways to do this are through dreams and active imagination. Roberto Gambini, in his book *Soul and Culture,* has a section on preschool children's art, which is a form of active imagination. You can see in the examples what the child has to deal with because their unconscious comes through in their art.

Our society puts a premium on conscious activity, like "I am married" and "I am a doctor". This is understandable because in order to be effective you need to be conscious of what you're doing and how you're feeling. Nevertheless, if you are unconscious of the factors we explain in this book these parts are not accessible. For example, Jung once forgot who he was while walking down a stairwell until he saw his name and profession imprinted on his door. This gave him the realization, "That's me!". The truth often manifests or breaks through as we saw in Jung's experience. Changes in relationship and vocation are commonly related to this as well.

Archetypes

These are inborn, basic types or imprints. Archetypes, which means 'ancient types', were originally postulated by Plato. They refer to ancient characteristics of everything in the world. For example, there are male, female, family, home, mother, father, and human archetypes. We can look at the mother archetype to see how this manifests. The mother archetype relates to anything feminine that is dealt with by anyone; not just women. For example, I once dreamt that I gave birth, which would fall into this category. I took this dream to mean that a new aspect of my personality was coming to life. All people have a certain amount of maternal instincts. In other words, every person can identify with the anima, which means 'soul' in Latin. For instance, someones unexpressed feminine characteristics often are manifested in their partner. But individuation occurs when that is withdrawn from the partner and integrated into one's own personality. This means that the individual likes, admires, and loves their self. Plus, they are ready to deal with what was previously unknown that is not yet conscious. Dreams often guide us in this process. We will delve deeper and discern such dreams in a later section of this book. In addition, active imagination, which we will also discuss later, leads to creative artistic products which always manifest various archetypes.

Complexes

Complexes are rooted in unsung conflicts. For instance, the ego complex, which we all have, is about our real and ideal sense of ourselves. Often, these are so different that they manifest as psychopathology. If we don't realize these inner aspects we will project them onto outer figures. Many times the projections are on people in leadership positions. But when we can put these aspects of ourselves together in a meaningful way and bring them into consciousness, they lead to self-realization, self-actualization, and individuation. How does this happen? Many times it's through family, friendships, therapy, and analysis. However, people are often apprehensive, or simply unaware, of the process of integrating an unconscious part of themselves. Resolution of these issues allows the individual to head down the path toward wholeness and achieve his or her objectives.

Every complex is related to an archetype. For instance, one's own difficulty with his or her own mother relates to the Great Mother archetype. In developing a relationship with this archetype we can birth and nurture our true selves. The same thing happens with the father. These allow us to have relationships, including with our own shadow figures, which are repressed figures of the same sex, positive or negative. Friends often represent parts of our own shadow. As an example, a childhood goal of mine was to be a minister, probably based on the admiration I had for a Unitarian minister. Later on in life, I became friends with someone who was a Quaker minister. The bottom line of this whole thing is that you have to love and accept yourself. This comes from being loved by parents, grandparents, friends, coworkers, and therapists. Through experiencing this, we can learn to love those parts of ourselves and others.

Anima and Animus

Anima in latin means 'soul'. In Jung's terms, the anima in a man represents the feminine side of himself. If he's unaware of this, he may unconsciously project it onto a woman. This creeps into the culture. Marilyn Monroe was an example of a collective projection of the feminine. Animus in latin means 'spirit'. In Jung's terms, it is the masculine side of a woman. A cultural example of a collective projection of the masculine was Elvis Presley. However, in reality both Marilyn Monroe and Elvis Presley had both soul and spirit, but split by the culture, they were unable to balance those and accept both of those aspects of themselves.

In a neuroanatomical sense, human beings have both masculine and feminine. In our current time these tend to be more manifested individually and culturally than they were in the past, such as when Jung was developing these terms in Switzerland many years ago. In another sense, people aren't as restricted to specific gender roles and stereotypes as they were. Graphic examples of this occur in medicine and the military. When I was in medical school, 5% of medical doctors were women. Now, it's thankfully 50%. The same kind of thing has happened in the military.

Syzygy

The concept of syzygy means both feminine and masculine, which is an overarching concept in everyone. Just as we have a representative of a mother archetype, we also have a representative of a father archetype. Both are important from the beginning. The maternal aspect gives birth, nurturance, and caring. The paternal aspect gives authority and knowledge. It's important to say that we all have both and that they are equally part of the *human* archetype. I say this so that they're not separate, or split, which unfortunately happens in our culture and many others. Surely this happened to Jung when he developed these concepts. Having both these archetypes leads to individuation and wholeness, or a holistic approach to life. Accepting the syzygy in oneself can lead to an inner marriage and a healthy coupling in the long-term sense. However, the inner marriage of masculine and feminine, spirit and soul, starts with oneself. Having this inner marriage can lead to more and better outer relationships.

Ego

The ego means "I" or the self identity (different from Self - this will be expanded on later). Often, the repressed aspect of one's identity is split off as are the defenses (as outlined in a lovely little book by Anna Freud). Part of the nature of in-depth therapy is to bring that split part back to the person as part of their wholeness. Ego psychology, which is prominent in our institutions and training, just focuses on the ego, which is like the American philosophy of "look out for number one." If you are just focused on individuality and not the familial, social, cultural, and spiritual aspects of relationships and life then you are cut off from a full life, which tragically is not that uncommon in the United States and the western world. Fortunately, Jung had the idea to place the ego consciousness secondary to the Self.

Shadow

This is the repressed aspect of one's identity that is split off. To use the example of a surgeon, the impulse to cut can be put in the service of healing. However, if the surgeon is not conscious of this it could become problematic. In writer and surgeon Richard Selzer's books, he comments on this. Once, he accidentally cut off the wrong leg of a patient. But because of his honesty in dealing with his own shadow and sharing this fact with the patient, he was forgiven by this person and he also worked on this for himself.

When the shadow is split off and unrecognized it could lead to war. War is really a product of collective shadow that is not recognized and accepted. For example, the enemy comes to represent a collective shadow which theoretically justifies the actions. We've all heard the stories of people who served in wars who say that there was actually no difference between themselves and the people they were supposed to kill or capture. I recall a story about soldiers in Texas during World War II who were in charge of a prison for captured enemies. They said that once they got to know their prisoners they realized that they were just like themselves. So, war is justified by creating a collective shadow.

Just as the negative shadow can be split off, the positive shadow can be split off too. Most people don't recognize the positive aspects that are repressed in themselves. In my own case, early on I did not realize that I was a writer and painter. Over time, these healing activities have been incorporated as part of my identity by owning and expressing these split off parts through active imagination and artistic products.

The Self Archetype

The Self archetype is related to a divinity or Supreme Being and represents wholeness. The ego is secondary to the Self. In ego psychology, people can get caught up in ego matters and thinking that they are ultimately in charge. When one is able to experience the ego, or personal self, as secondary to the Self or Supreme Being, then they are able to be a part of a spiritual process and find meaning, purpose, humility, and relief in their life. That is why a Jungian psychoanalyst can see all people and embrace their different religious practices. All paths lead up the mountain to the summit. Abraham Maslow knew this when he postulated about self-actualization and that a link to the spirit and soul is the culmination of a long and difficult journey. This journey is often reflected in storytelling, whether in analysis, memoir, or novels.

The Self archetype is often represented by a mandala, which manifests as a circle and is a symbol of wholeness. This is illustrated particularly in the last two artistic products in the section on *Active Imagination*. In looking at the four artistic products in this section, you can see from my own evolution that the circles were there at the beginning, but they developed more fully as the journey of individuation proceeded. Healing is an ongoing process. One is never fully developed, as we are always struggling and growing. That is why I went back into therapeutic analysis in my seventies.

Numinous

Numinous in Latin means 'divine will'. What is this divinity? Some people say it's God, or Goddess, which makes sense because it separates human from divine. This leads to the question, "How do we discover our divine nature?" Children don't have a problem with this because they quickly see and accept themselves and others as unique and related to something special. Why is this often not there in adults? We must dig deeper and get back to our divine children within. Our divine children within come from our divine inner parents, or the Great Mother and Great Father. This is the link to the numinous. It's interesting to note that the Mayans included not only the concept of divine parents, but also divine grandparents and other relatives.

Numinous also has to do with finding light in darkness. In other words, we are always looking for hope in hopeless situations and courage in situations in which we are afraid. So, the numinous allows us to see in the dark. This underscores why I feel darkness and depression are so important. We must master the light going out. Children naturally do this and even play games regarding it. Blind people are forced to do this. It is important for us as adults to venture out in the darkness, with our cell phones or flash lights if need be. However, once you know the path, you ought to be able to venture on it without any accessories.

Gnosis

Gnosis, in ancient Greek, means 'to know'. A Gnostic, therefore, is one who knows. Who knows what? The essence of oneself, which is the true self. This true self includes both feminine and masculine aspects of personality. In fact, the Gnostic church, which still exists today, portrays the Supreme Being as feminine. They have long had women as equal to men in leadership positions. Socrates knew about this concept of self-knowledge with his philosophy of "Know thyself". This is the essence of any self-realization and therapy. Any person in therapy or analysis has to be involved in this process, or it won't work. However, most people are not aware of this because they reflect the split culture, which divides female and male and projects unconscious parts of themselves onto others. Those who want to be effective therapists or analysts also have to deal with this in themselves. Hippocrates, the man considered to be the father of medicine said, "Physician, heal thyself". This concept also appears in the Bible and many other spiritual writings. Giving birth to your true self means that you have transformed the false self and given equal weight to the masculine and feminine.

Typology

Typology was Jung's way of dealing with his own personality. For instance, we are born either introverted or extraverted. This is the first axis of typology and refers to one's attitude in the world. These terms came from Jung and he dealt with both of them in himself and others. The task of our development is to incorporate the opposite. For example, Jung went from being a shy and introverted person to expressing his extraversion through healing others, teaching, and writing.

The second axis refers to sensing or intuition. Sensing relates to the facts. It comes from sensation. In Jung's case, he would have had to have sensing to go to the university. Intuition is different from sensing in that it has to do more with imagination. It's kind of like a sixth sense. Children often express intuition. If you ask a child if they can fly, they may say, "Sure! Can't you?" Jung exhibited his own flying ability by developing his unique psychology, which was flying away from Freud and toward his mother and father, who exhibited a love of mythology and religion.

Another axis of typology is thinking and feeling. Jung developed both of these aspects. His thinking function, like sensing, allowed him to excel in school. It would be almost impossible to go to medical school if you hadn't developed the thinking aspect of your typology. His feeling nature allowed him to relate well with patients and others that he contacted through his life. The feeling function can be a more difficult one to embrace because it does not refer to just "I feel good" or "I feel bad". Rather, it has to do with connection and evaluating through one's heart and soul.

A goal for all of us in life is to move toward wholeness, which involves incorporating all six of these functions: introversion and extraversion, sensing and intuition, and thinking and feeling. One of the reasons I identified with Jung was because I have been working on these same things during my life.

Symbols

Why have a separate section on these aspects of life? Because symbols are critically important to Jung's Analytical Psychology. They're different from signs in that symbols can stand for many things. Symbols are linked to creativity. In other words, there are very few creative aspects of a stop *sign*. However, if you talk about a stop *symbol*, there would be a many. The sun is a symbol of wholeness and a source of everything. But if you stare at it you'll go blind. That would be a stop symbol: "Stop it!"

I'll give some examples of meaningful symbols. The first one is the Star of David, which is made up of two triangles. The triangle itself is a symbol. It is grounded and reaching to the stars. So, it mixes the two aspects of reality: the earth and sky. The Star of David also has a triangle pointing downward. So, it has one triangle pointing up and one pointing down. It is an integration of feminine and masculine, of earth and sky. This symbol is not limited to Judaism. You'll find a similar image in Hinduism and Shintoism. This shows how symbols are universal.

Another meaningful symbol is the cross. However, it's not limited to Christianity. It's meaning lies in that one pole is vertical, integrating Mother Earth and Father Sky, and the other pole is horizontal, which parallels the surface of the planet. However, they can be placed inside of a circle, such as in a sun cross, which gives a sense of wholeness and is more feminine. The circle is a symbol of the feminine and a triangle the symbol of the masculine. This is illustrated in kinship charts.

What's interesting is that two triangles makes the Star of David, and two circles makes the mandorla, an almond-shaped symbol. The almond links it to a tree that's grounded in the earth and reaches to the sky. The lens shape of the mandorla symbolizes sight, and insight. The mandorla is a numinous symbol as it also signifies light. So, again, the symbol is grounded in the Earth and also reaches for the light above.

Dreams

Often, when we wake from a dream we wonder, "What did that mean?" The psyche provides these doors of insight to help us enter the lands of conflicts and goals. Fortunately, dream analysis is part of Jungian psychology. After years of dealing with my own dreams and the dreams of others I've come to realize that these are prophetic and cosmic gifts from the Maker that allow us to understand ourselves and others. Sadly, dreams are often tossed away as meaningless. However, we know from the words of others that these messages can lead to creation and transformation. This is what happened to Jung when he left Freud and developed his own healing way. Jung expanded Freud's view of the personal unconscious to postulate the collective unconscious, which is based on the evolution of everything, thus embracing wholeness. Another quite different example is August Kekele, who discovered in a dream the benzene ring which is the basis of organic chemistry, biochemistry, and therefore medicine. This also happened to Isaac Singer when he dreamt about the sewing machine. Did he invent it or was it a gift from the Creator that he was the midwife for?

It's meaningful to also reflect on dreams being a central part of all religions. However, Freud thought that they were mostly based on personal issues having to do with sex and aggression. Why would this be the case? Because we receive helpful clues and images from them. Dreams have symbolic meanings, and we analyze and understand them through association and amplification. To help the reader, after the next section I give examples of these images and symbols from my own dreams and in-depth work. The old adage, "seeing is believing" is true. One way we can amplify dreams as counselors, therapists, and analysts, is to encourage ourselves and our patients to follow the dream by drawing or painting it. This process is called active imagination. Just like all creative processes, it leads to self-discovery.

Active Imagination

Carl Jung was a gifted artist, physician, and in-depth therapist. These attributes were part of his character. For example, long before he was a psychoanalyst, he created both realistic landscapes and later, mandalas as well as more abstract impressions. His unique, autobiographical writing, *The Red Book*, provides evidence of his artistic ability and meaningful associations. Through active imagination, we create artistic products that involve significant connections related to one's life journey and the evolutionary history of the collective.

In the late 1980's, I was visiting Franz Jung, Jung's son, who was living in the actual house of his parents in

Kusnacht, Switzerland. He invited me into Jung's personal office and library. I was touched and moved to be there. Often, pictures of Jung are from times that he spent in this office. It was his creative sanctuary. In a naive way, I said to Franz, "What does this Red Book look like?" He said, "Oh, it's right here." We both looked through it and thought it was brilliant and magical. We talked about how maybe it was left so that the family could facilitate the birth of this creative work. At that time though, Franz was uncertain whether it would be released to the public because his father didn't directly say what to do with it. But, I wondered then and now why he left it with his only son. Eventually, because the family was so impressed with the work they all got together and decided that it should be published. So, what they were doing was providing the world with what Carl Jung had created. Many of Jung's illustrations are published not just in *The Red Book*, but online as well. They're available for the public to observe and find their own meaning in these self-reflective illustrations.

Jung viewed one's own illness as related to one's personal myth and one's ability to create. In other words, he viewed one's sickness as creative. This asks the question, "Why are we here and what are we meant to create?" This way of creating something new is the essence of death and rebirth. Something has to die, but through that death experience the energy is available for something new which is characteristic of that unique individual. Children naturally do this. They don't hesitate to create new things. Also, when one thinks back to preschool and kindergarten, that's when the essence of the person was often recognized. Many times, this was obvious to parents, family members, and teachers. On the following pages are examples of spontaneous products from my own dreams and active imagination. They also capture the idea of transforming my own difficulties into something new, creative, and unique related to my personal myth, which is related to the wounded healer.

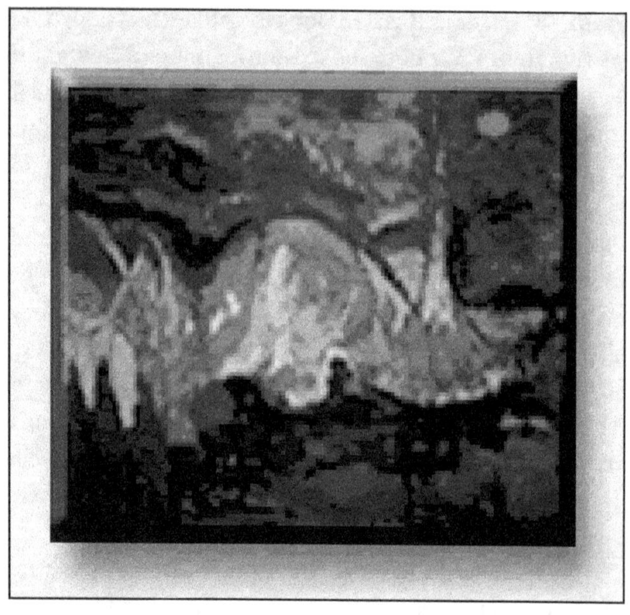

Emotional Landscape, 1966

I painted this the the year that I entered medical school, which was a rewarding but stressful experience. Quickly, it's apparent that there's a lot of deep, dark, water I had to enter and learn to swim in along with peaks I had to climb. To be told in the first year of med school that we have to cut on a dead human being in order to comprehend the complexity of human anatomy was shocking and humbling. However, in this painting, there's also movement and ascendency, or a reaching beyond or above. This was my early struggle of trying to figure out what was going on and why I was entering medicine. However, I was never able to leave it. That's why, in 2017, Oxford University Press published *Patient-Centered Medicine: A Human Experience.* This text was co-authored with a former student, Uyen Hoang. Of course, now I realize that this painting reflects self-healing. Ironically, this was one of my first oil paintings, which was done on a piece of plywood that I had found in my garage. So, whenever we say to ourselves or patients say to us, "I can't paint, write poetry, or take original photographs" it's not true. My own experience with my personal struggles and those with patients reveal that everybody wants to create art and tell their own stories. In fact, it refreshes one's body and soul.

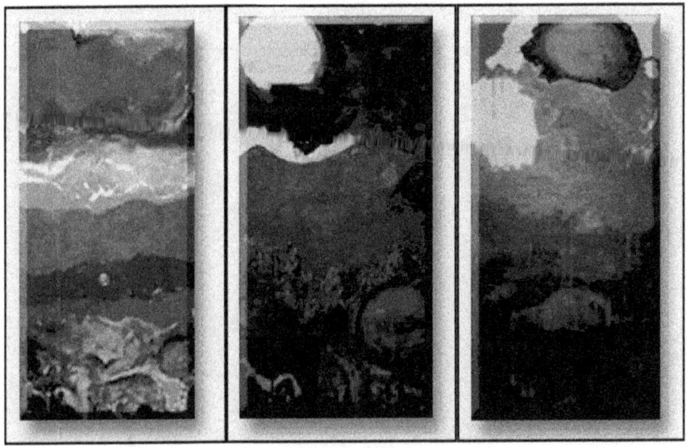

1967, 1968, 1969
Triptych

I also did these paintings during my time in medical school. They were made, as all artistic products are, to promote one's mental health and psychic balance. To say the least, medical school was difficult, but rewarding. You can see that in the paintings. The bottom of the two paintings on the right are dark for depression and the conflicts of illness and death. There is also green in the paintings for nature. The middle part in the two paintings on the right are red, yellow, and orange, which often suggests caution and danger. Going to medical school allowed me to have an experience with very ill and dying patients, which probably relates to my own despair and search for sunshine and blue skies. It's clear to me that the bright colors indicate that my soul was striving for wholeness.

I had seen an ad in the newspaper for these canvases. When I went to look at them, the person told me that they were beds for little children in preschool. I was struck by this fact because as children, we spontaneously draw and paint. So, what I was doing in an unconscious way was linking my struggles to that time in my life.

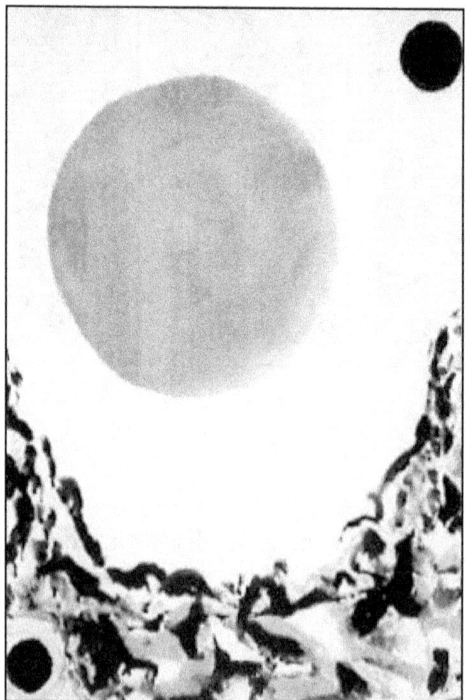

The Tao of Jung, 1993

Being a Jungian in an academic Psychology department for 25 years was challenging and had it's own unique stress. This painting was done at a time when I was writing a book by the same name, *The Tao of Jung*, which was published a few years later. It's all about centering and balance. The golden mandala in the center, which is also the sun, represents the source of everything. It's going to be joined with the scenes of nature below. The two black circles illustrate the nigredo (which represents melancholia and/or depression, as well as a source of healing). Hence, that led to my writing the book *Transforming Depression: Healing the Soul Through Creativity*, which was published this same year.

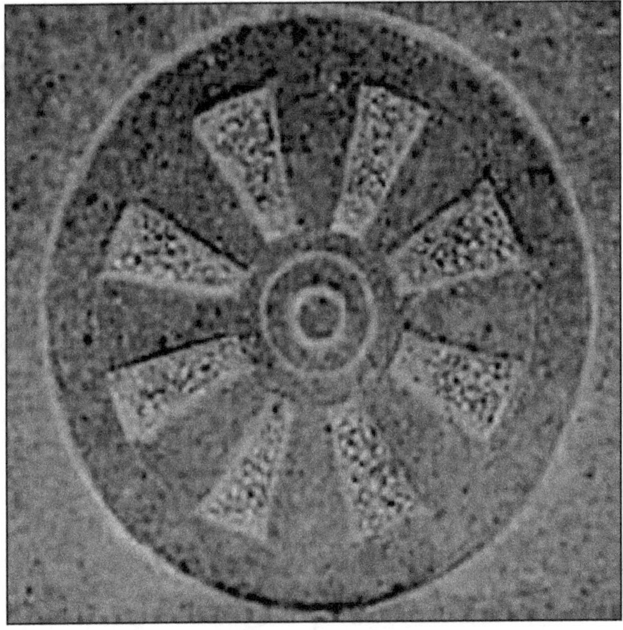

Carved Stone Mandala, 2003

I engaged in active imagination in Italy at the Santa Chiara campus of Texas A&M University. The sculptor who I took lessons from lived in a nearby village. Faculty and students were able to attend this campus, which was the former nunnery of Saint Claire, the platonic lover of Saint Francis. There are four mandalas and eight spokes within this carving. The mandalas represent wholeness and the number eight, in numerology, relates to inner-strength, self-confidence, and a peaceful nature. Circles are feminine and symbols of wholeness. I had recently been through a divorce with the mother of my three daughters. However, in a meaningful way, at this time I was married to myself. What I mean by this is I loved myself. I recall my parents once telling me, "When you love yourself, everything will be all right." This was a time of self-discovery and meaningful relationships with students and faculty in a setting that was conducive to healing.

Egocide and Transcendence

I have a specialization in the area of suicidal depression, which I'm sure stems in part from my own issues regarding this condition. The best expert opinion about something is someone who has gone through the same process themselves. In our society, suicide is a critical topic. For example, in the June 2022 issue of *The Journal of Analytical Psychology*, there was an article titled "Self, ego and suicide" by Oliver Dale of London. I was pleasantly surprised to find this in the journal because this is such an important topic that is not usually discussed there. The article even cited the research I did with Golden Gate bridge survivors. That study brought home the fact that the ego was the real culprit. Because of this, as a meaningful alternative to suicide, I developed the concept of egocide. I realized that people who are wanting to kill themselves get confused. What they really want to kill is their concept of the suicidal self. In my research, I found that this is what happened to the people who survived jumping off the Golden Gate bridge. The survivors experienced a death and rebirth.

The ego will come up with the idea that the person wants to kill themselves. Instead, one can kill the suicidal part of their ego that wants to end their life. This can be done by analyzing that part of themselves to death. The benefits of such an activity led to Betty Ford, the wife of former President Gerald Ford, to analyze to death the part of her ego that was drinking herself to death. The process of egocide is similar to Alcoholics Anonymous. In fact, Betty Ford went through this process herself at a Navy based rehab center, which brings a truth and reality to her experience. I also use this therapeutic treatment in my own work helping patients experience egocide, transcendence, and transformation. This is the same as the death and rebirth experience which is so common in Jungian therapy and psychoanalysis.

Transcendent Function

Once the individual realizes their split off parts of their self and Self, they can incorporate that into their identity. Often, this happens in vivid dreams and/or creative activities because they can then see it, just like our common philosophy "seeing is believing". This transcendence commonly occurs because of a repressed transcendent function which allows one to go beyond the conflict. It is like a guiding principle or star. In Betty Ford's case, she was able to take her experience of egocide and transcendence in her own life and use that to establish the Betty Ford centers, which surely have helped many people to deal with their addictions. An opposite kind of case is Elvis Presley, who was unable to do what Betty Ford did and ended up going further and further into his addiction and eventually ended up dying of complications associated with it. I explain these opposite approaches to personal conflicts in *Transforming Depression: Healing the Soul Through Creativity*.

Transformation

To sum up the process of personal awareness and transformation, I like to think of what Paul Tillich said, "Estranged and reunited, the new being." All one's confession and in-depth work to understand oneself leads to the birth of one's Real self, like Maslow discussed in his writings and Jung embodied and lived. Surely, this was why I wrote the book *Transforming Depression: Healing the Soul Through Creativity*. As we have seen in the section on active imagination, this new being results from putting all the pieces together. It's like a puzzle that you work hard on and then all of the sudden you begin to see the core and one's character emerge. Once the therapist or analyst goes through this change, it's possible to help others go down this same, unpaved road. When you get to the end, you realize that there's really often no need for pavement. You can accept the Earth and the gravel as the truth. Often, the pavement came into existence because we needed to go faster to get places. However, it's vital to stay at home, which is in your heart and soul and realize the gift and beauty of your own humanity.

Individuation

Individuation, like self-realization, is the culmination of one's development through insight and doing one's best to become whole. It's a unique term because Jung did not mean *individualism,* which is an American virtue. He meant *individuation,* which is meant to be figuring out one's own personal myth and how one provides service to themselves and others. As our friend and Nobel laureate, Bob, Dylan, said, "You're gonna have to serve somebody." It's important to make the distinction between individualism and individuation, which Jung was careful to clarify. Individuation, or the journey toward wholeness, is never realized. However, the nectar is in the journey. This allows the novice to deal with the shadow, anima, and animus, and whatever aspects of one's personality would contribute to the development of one's personal myth. Individuation encompasses work, play, relationships, and finding meaning. It is the summation of one's life. Likewise, it is the culmination of Jung's psychology.

Bringing This to a Close

I developed two courses at Texas A&M that reflect my own development which has been influenced by Frank N. McMillan, Jr., Frank N. McMillan III, and Jung himself. The first was "Psychology of Self" in which students would hear and see through my sharing personal history about my life, growth, development, and transformation. In the other course, "Psychology of Religion", students would hear about my own bridging from ego to find spiritual meaning. Part of these courses involved students sharing their own stories about themselves and their religion, which was terrifying to most of them. One student who was selected actually fainted. Later, they recovered and thought it was a good idea to talk about themselves to the class. It allowed for these experiences to be acknowledged and reflected on by various individuals in the classes. So, we built on our unique selves and learned to share it, which was respectful of differences. How refreshing!

A Final Word

My whole life prepared me to meet Lanara in New Zealand. My father, a world traveler, once told me, "Be sure you go to New Zealand at some point in your life." I said, "Why?" He responded, "That country is the most beautiful and civilized one in the world." I was shocked that there would be any country that could fit those parameters, so I said to myself, "I'm gonna go there."

A score of years later, I decided to take one of my sabbaticals, which is one of the best gifts of being a professor, at the University of Canterbury in Christchurch, on the south island of New Zealand. In a small way, going there honored the memory of my father, and he was correct in what he said about the country. While there, I lived in a little village, Governors Bay. Being high up on a hill I could see the view in the picture below daily. I remember telling relatives and friends that this was the most aesthetic place I've ever been.

Governors Bay

Often, I would drive to Allendale Reserve (which is what we call in the United States a park) to have my lunch on a bench that overlooked Governors Bay and then go on a walk to the jetty. One day, I drove there and to my surprise, there was a woman sitting on the bench. I could tell that the way she was sitting meant, "Don't sit here". However, given my brazen personality and liking the same view, I asked her in a gentle way to please move over so that I could sit down and enjoy my lunch while looking at the view. She took her time in answering. Finally, she said, "Sure, it's alright" and moved over. So, I sat down next to her. After I ate, I told her that I was going to walk to the jetty and back. She replied, "Me too." So, I responded with that great phrase when you fall in love with somebody, "Would it be okay for me to walk with you?" The subsequent silence was longer than anyone would expect. Eventually, she responded, "That'll be fine."

The walkway we went on used to be an old stagecoach road. It went right along the water and then ended up in Governors Bay. This afforded me the opportunity to ask her questions, such as her name, which she told me was Lanara. Because I had not heard that name before but liked it a lot, it was burned into my memory. Later, I found out that Lanara was a minor goddess in Bergonian mythology who represented beauty and vanity. Vanity has a questionable connotation to most people, however it means self-acceptance and love. We even shared phone numbers, and I said, "Give me a call and we could have dinner sometime." She didn't call, so I rang her. We ended up walking many times on the same pathway. In order to learn more about her, I asked her over to my hillside place several times and made various dinners for her.

When it was time for me to fly back to Texas, I was in the Qantas line about to board the airplane and I asked her if she would like to marry me. She said, "Let me think about it." I returned to New Zealand two more times, and the reason was her. It took four years for her to finally agree to marry me. Meeting Lanara on a bench halfway across the world is a clear example of synchronicity, that meaningful, acausal connection that we are all looking for. And being married to Lanara is an act of individuation.